3/14

Great Women in History

Susan B. Anthony

by Erin Edison

Consulting Editor: Gail Saunders-Smith, PhD

Consultant: Dr. Brie Swenson Arnold
Assistant Professor of History
Coe College, Cedar Rapids, Iowa

CAPSTONE PRESS
a capstone imprint

Pebble Books are published by Capstone Press,
1710 Roe Crest Drive, North Mankato, Minnesota 56003.
www.capstonepub.com

Library of Congress Cataloging-in-Publication Data
Edison, Erin.
  Susan B. Anthony / by Erin Edison.
    p. cm.—(Pebble books. Great women in history)
  Includes bibliographical references and index.
  ISBN 978-1-62065-075-2 (library binding)
  ISBN 978-1-62065-865-9 (paperback)
  ISBN 978-1-4765-1631-8 (eBook PDF)
  1. Anthony, Susan B. (Susan Brownell), 1820–1906—Juvenile literature.
  2. Suffragists—United States—Biography—Juvenile literature. 3. Feminists—
United States—Biography—Juvenile literature. 4. Women's rights—United
States—Juvenile literature. I. Title.
HQ1413.A55E35 2013
305.42092—dc23
[B]   2012033475

Note to Parents and Teachers

The Great Women in History set supports national social studies
standards related to people and culture. This book describes and
illustrates Susan B. Anthony. The images support early readers in
understanding the text. The repetition of words and phrases helps
early readers learn new words. This book also introduces early
readers to subject-specific vocabulary words, which are defined
in the Glossary section. Early readers may need assistance to read
some words and to use the Table of Contents, Glossary, Read More,
Internet Sites, and Index sections of the book.

Printed in the United States of America in Stevens Point, Wisconsin.
092012   006937WZS13

Table of Contents

1820

born

Early Life

Susan Brownell Anthony worked for the rights of women. Susan was born February 15, 1820, in Adams, Massachusetts. Her parents were Daniel and Lucy Anthony.

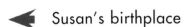

Susan's birthplace

1820
born

1826
Anthony family
moves to New York

6

Susan's family moved to New York in 1826. She went to school there. She later went to boarding school in Pennsylvania.

Anthony home in Battenville, New York, built in 1833

1820
born

1826
Anthony family
moves to New York

1838
becomes a
teacher

1849
moves to Rochester,
New York

Young Adult

Susan became a teacher in 1838. Teaching was one of the few jobs for women at this time. Susan was a strict but skilled teacher.

In 1849 Susan moved to Rochester, New York. She quit teaching to become a reformer.

 1820

born

 1826

Anthony family
moves to New York

1838

becomes a
teacher

1849

moves to Rochester,
New York

Reformers work to change things they think are wrong. At the time, slavery was common in southern states. Slaves had to work without pay. Susan thought slavery was wrong. She also thought drinking alcohol should be against the law.

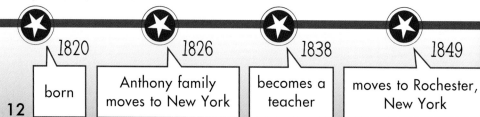

1820 — born

1826 — Anthony family moves to New York

1838 — becomes a teacher

1849 — moves to Rochester, New York

Susan went to meetings about slavery and alcohol. But the men wouldn't let her speak because she was a woman.

1852

is not allowed to speak at a meeting

1820 born

1826 Anthony family moves to New York

1838 becomes a teacher

1849 moves to Rochester, New York

Life's Work

At the time, most women weren't allowed to own property. Women often weren't allowed to work outside the home. If they did work, they didn't earn as much money as men. Women also couldn't vote. Susan wanted rights for women.

1852

is not allowed to speak at a meeting

1820
born

1826
Anthony family
moves to New York

1838
becomes a
teacher

1849
moves to Rochester,
New York

Susan worked closely with women's rights reformer Elizabeth Cady Stanton. They gathered men and women together to talk about woman suffrage. The right to vote is called suffrage.

1852

is not allowed to speak at a meeting

1820
born

1826
Anthony family
moves to New York

1838
becomes a
teacher

1849
moves to Rochester,
New York

Susan and Elizabeth gave speeches, held meetings, and wrote books and articles. They wanted to bring attention to woman suffrage. Susan worked for women's rights her entire life.

1852
is not allowed to
speak at a meeting

1870s
goes on
speaking tour

1820
born

1826
Anthony family
moves to New York

1838
becomes a
teacher

1849
moves to Rochester,
New York

Remembering Susan

Susan died in 1906. Congress

passed the 19th Amendment

in 1920. This law is known as

the Susan B. Anthony Amendment.

It says women can vote.

Susan's work has given millions

of women this important right.

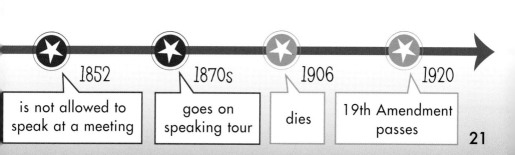

1852 — is not allowed to speak at a meeting

1870s — goes on speaking tour

1906 — dies

1920 — 19th Amendment passes

Glossary

amendment—a formal change made to a law or legal document, such as the U.S. Constitution

boarding school—a school that students live in during the school year

Congress—the branch of the U.S. government that makes laws

reformer—a person who works to bring about change for a large group of people; reformers often want to change laws or have new laws made

right—what the law says people can have or do

slavery—the owning of other people; slaves are forced to work without pay

suffrage—the right to vote

Read More

Boothroyd, Jennifer. *Susan B. Anthony: A Life of Fairness.* Biographies. Minneapolis: Lerner Publications, 2006.

Slade, Suzanne. *Susan B. Anthony: Fighter for Freedom and Equality.* Biographies. Minneapolis: Picture Window Books, 2007.

Wallner, Alexandra. *Susan B. Anthony.* New York: Holiday House, 2011.

Internet Sites

FactHound offers a safe, fun way to find Internet sites related to this book. All of the sites on FactHound have been researched by our staff.

Here's all you do:

Visit *www.facthound.com*

Type in this code: 9781620650752

Super-cool stuff! Check out projects, games and lots more at **www.capstonekids.com**

Index

Word Count: 277
Grade: 1
Early-Intervention Level: 25

Editorial Credits

Erika L. Shores, editor; Alison Thiele, designer; Wanda Winch, media researcher; Jennifer Walker, production specialist

Photo Credits

Corbis: Bettmann, 16, 18; Courtesy of the Department of Rare Books and Special Collections, University of Rochester Library, 8; Getty Images Inc/Bridgeman Art Library/William Aiken Walker, 10; Library of Congress: Prints and Photographs Division, cover, 1, 4, 14, 20; Photo Researchers, Inc., 12; Shutterstock: Christophe Boisson, cover design; Susan B. Anthony House, 6